Interwoven

Dear Shahdan,

Let's stay
Interwoven.

♡

Sarina.

Interwoven

Serina D'Cruz Lewis

TAMARIND TREE BOOKS
Toronto

Tamarind Tree Books Inc.,
info@tamarindtreebooks.ca.
ttb.imprint@gmail.com
OR
Serina D'Cruz Lewis,
serinadcruzlewis@gmail.com

Library and Archives Canada Cataloguing in Publication

Title: Interwoven / Serina D'Cruz Lewis.
Names: Lewis, Serina D'Cruz, author.
Description: Includes index.
Identifiers: Canadiana 20240478568 | ISBN 9781989242162 (softcover)
Subjects: LCGFT: Poetry.
Classification: LCC PS8623.E9686 I58 2024 | DDC C811/.6—dc23

Editor: Zilka Joseph; Cover design: Rudi Rodrigues; Author Photo: Noel Lewis

DEDICATION

to

my fellow travelers
straddling continents
on their journey
whose stories are
intricately interwoven

In Praise Of 'Interwoven'

'Interwoven' is a masterfully crafted poetic memoir that resonated deeply with me. The poet's tribute to her ancestors by honoring their "integrity, sincerity, and struggles during hardships" sets a spiritual tone. Her journey as an immigrant is profoundly moving with poems that explore themes of identity, culture, food, migration, and belonging.

Her ability to craft beautiful language through perfect word choice is evident. 'The Circle' is a marvelous tribute to humanity as a whole; amongst the weavers of tales she includes the toddy tappers and those in "humble *chappals*". Through an interesting stanza layout, the reader may feel a constant movement adding people from all walks of life;

> *"enlarging the ever-widening sphere*
> *the circle -- with no definite circumference" paints a visual image.*

'Fresh off the Boat' tells the story of migration, both personal and universal. As an immigrant myself, I deeply relate to the apprehensions and risks described;

> *"Our bridges burn*
> *no taking U-turns*
> *blood, sweat and tears*
> *faith, joy and fears"*

In a few short poems she masterfully weaves together her parents' biography from their 'Arranged Marriage' to the poignant end of their lifespan, in 'My Way' a heart-wrenching tribute to her father, the poet's emotions resonate as she grapples with his mortality.

> *"Was I driftwood floating?*
> *or a black box sinking?"*

Her vivid imagery transported me back to my own father's final days. I shed a few tears. Her masterpiece poem 'Singer' is skillfully interwoven with childhood memories. A moving tribute, 'My Mother's Hands' that bathed and bundled, but sometimes punished her and her siblings with

> *"a vice-like grip to keep us in our place".*

The poet's ability to balance praise with honest vulnerability is a testament to her skill and emotional depth. The vivid poems about her siblings and offspring will take you back to your personal experiences.

Through poems about the culinary delights of our Eastern cuisine, I was transported to the stall of 'Phuchkas of Kolkata' (*Gole Gappay*).

Each poem is a journey that transports me to new destinations, whether by train, plane, or river. 'Waters' is a perfect example with her ever-gripping opening lines;

In Praise Of 'Interwoven'

"From life-giving waters I broke out
A foetus emerged
from a dark constricted tunnel
into the bright wide world"

'Half and Half' is a great ending to this migration story —32 years in the East and 32 years in Canada.

This collection is a grand symphony of emotions, with each poem flowing into the next to create a lasting impression. The poet's love for her "chosen homeland" shines through in her tribute to Canada's beauty, acknowledging the Indigenous experience and drawing parallels between colonization and migration. In conclusion, 'Interwoven' is a masterpiece collection that has left me speechless. I salute Serina for enriching the world of poetry with her passionate and thought-provoking work. I'm honored to have reviewed this collection and wish for many more years of her valuable contributions to the world of poetry.

— *Zohra Zoberi is an award-winning poet, author and playwright. She is bi-lingual and her memoir entitled "The Other I" traces her fascinating migration story that connects East and West. Two books to her credit are "True Colours" and "Questionably Ever After" and most recently she co-authored a book called "One and One Make Eleven".*

❧ ✳ ✳ ✳ ✳ ✳ ✳ ✳ ✳ ✳ ✳ ✳ ✳

Serina D'Cruz Lewis writes of family, migration, perseverance and fortitude in Interwoven. This collection of stirring works will resonate with anyone who has migrated and struggled to establish a new life—and triumphed. These poems also pay homage to those who came before: ancestors who would be proud and delighted to learn that their descendants have continued on to lead lives of love, support and respect. Some of the works have poetic forms that skillfully reflect their topics; for instance, the echoes of a metaphorical heartbeat in "The Circle." Others employ rhyming quatrains or evocative blank verse. I found myself wanting to reach for a cup of "Chai" and a plate of the "Phuchkas of Kolkata," and I laughed alongside the family at the "In Mid-Air" predicament. This book gratifies the reader's curiosity, while being thoroughly entertaining. An emotional, engaging read.

— *Sheila E. Tucker: Author of 'Rag Dolls and Rage', and editor of anthologies 'Crazy Cove', 'Musings', and 'Things That Matter'.*

Invocation

Day of the Living

Today, I call upon my great-grandfather Caridade Rodrigues
    I call upon my great-grandmother Rita Rodrigues
    I call upon my great-grandfather Camilo Da Cruz
    I call my great-grandmother Ana Ditosa Da Cruz
    I call them great.
Their spirit of adventure
    of sincerity
    of integrity
    of tenacity
    of strength in times of colonization
        of struggle
        of hardship
        of scarcity
        of want
during world wars, drought, flood, and lack of basic livelihood
when the bottle of liquor was their best friend
when elders were their counselors, their solace and support.

I call upon the spirit of my Grandpa Salu
I call upon the spirit of Nana Bemvinda
I call upon the spirit of Granny Anna Gracia
I call upon the spirit of Grandpa C C Cruz
To thank them for warm memories of Christmas and New Year
        for delectable letri, bathica, dose and pinag
        for evening walks in the park and chapel courtyard
        for mannddem, dulpodam, and stories of travels
        for treats from street vendors and doting love
        for days long gone but cherished memories
    that linger in the soft folds of a child's brain.

{Contd.} Invocation

I call upon the soul of Mum Theresa
I call upon the soul of Dad Francis
I call upon the soul of Mum Bella
I call upon the soul of Dad Eddie
who bequeathed to us faith
                    patience
                    independence
                    determination

to a family of strong men
even stronger women
enterprising children
Remaining here with their endearing
                    sustaining
                    enveloping
                    strengthening presence around us.

If upon an ofrenda I place water
                    candles
                    flowers
                    pictures
                    homemade sweetmeats
I feel a shiver of energy run down my spine and
I know they never left-
have transitioned into
another land of the living.

CONTENTS

{01} The Circle

They gather around the circle
the maker of music
    the weaver of tales
        the grinder of spices
            the tiller of the rice fields
                the adventurer who sailed the seven seas
                    ancestors who walked barefoot
                    or in humble chappals
they gather by the fire
to stoke the flames of the hearts
of those still in the earth realm
Wandering this sansaar are
        the artists
          the writers
            the soldiers
              the bankers
                the teachers
              the. engineers
          the thinkers
Dhonnobad to all those who serve the human family

Let us not forget
the herbal healers
    the toddy tappers
      the tireless helpers
        the singers of mannddem
          the soothers of the lonely
            the dreamers of foreign shores
              the birthers of successive generations
                the youth who wrote letters for their elders
each one leaving footprints indelible on Mother Earth

{Contd.} The Circle

To the Ancient ones
    Spirit Guides
    Forefathers and Foremothers
waiting to welcome home my soul
from lands of the Mississaugas of the Credit
enlarging the ever-widening sphere
the circle—with no definite circumference
around the primordial fire at its heart

Miigwech Chi- Miigwech

{02} Fresh Off The Boat

Welcome to Toronto.
The time on arrival is…good
If you are in transit…proceed to
If you are staying….

Yes, we're arriving— not leaving
We're here to stay
Two adults with two children
Four suitcases and $800

Our bridges burned
No taking U-turns
Blood sweat and tears
Faith joys and fears

Whatever the future brings
Whichever way fortune swings
We're here in this new land
Will Lady Luck hold our hand?

Farewell to the land of our birth
Never doubting our decision's worth
Following an ancestor to foreign shores
Hoping for the opening of doors

Exhausted Intimidated
Undaunted Excited
Familiar faces shout hoorays
Waving a banner that says

Welcome to Canada!

{03} Blank Page

During the recession, I almost changed my profession
because it was more than just that- it was a vocation.
Dreaming of lands far away and experiences so different.
Dreams evaporated but courage prevailed—and I didn't.

If I had remained a small-town girl
with comfort and familiarity
I wouldn't have flown across the globe.
I almost stayed put—but I didn't.

I chose the boy from across the road
with big dreams and ambitions,
who crossed oceans and continents with me.
We almost gave up—but we didn't.

Had I let racism and nepotism weigh me down,
I would never have achieved what I have.
One step at a time covered mile after mile,
I almost stopped—but I didn't.

If I doubted that I could string words together,
Would I have been writing this today?
Often tempted to leave the page blank,
I almost did—but I didn't.

{04} Arranged Marriage

Who said that mom would be left on a shelf,
teaching and travel, laughter and singing,
none so brazen and sure of herself,
she'd spend her days, dancing and swinging.
> She went on a family conspired tour,
> hoping for sparks on that hill resort trip,
> following her closely went dad to allure,
> but missed meeting her and boy! did she flip.
Back to the drawing board he did return,
motivated by a special reason,
to plan another well-thought-out sojourn,
knowing she was his second cousin.
> Travelling by train to win her favour,
> Fingers crossed for love at first sight,
> to win a bride in this endeavour,
> as indeed it would be on that fateful night.
He was impressed by her hour-glass figure,
while she didn't notice he had two left feet,
with good looks, charm and apparent vigour,
a match was lit on the day they did meet.
> Getting acquainted by mail with each other
> their love letters couldn't arrive fast enough
> Parents made sure they didn't delay either
> details chalked out and all was set up.
Eddie and Bella's marriage was arranged,
blessed with showers on a summer's day,
Vows were read and rings exchanged
They were united for life on the third of May.

• Serina D'Cruz Lewis •

{05} My Way

For Dad who had two left feet

I was an adult orphan,
In my own company—so often.

All I could do was stare,
It was so difficult to bear,
Could I keep on living?
Could I understand dying?
Was I driftwood floating?
Or a black box sinking?

Listening to his favourite song,
I found myself singing along,
I remember gentle arms around me,
As we swayed together smoothly,
In a hospital gown, right beside his bed,
On a then bony shoulder, I laid my head.
Step by lingering step
Every beat Dad kept

It's like the sun's ray touches me
when I hear Sinatra sing—
"I Did It My Way".

{06} Last Effort

As a young boy in Goa,
barefoot playing soccer in dry rice paddies,
cuts and scrapes marked Dad's tender soles
corns and calluses hardened for skillful dribbling.

In World War days, by streetlight, he strained
his eyes to learn from engineering texts
to get a degree, though death and despair spread
like lava in Calcutta, during the British Raj.

What future was there in times of uncertainty?
work on Banbury machines, carbon lined his nostrils,
nicotine marks where countless cigarettes stained
the edges of fingers, and hands that laboured
to do whatever it took to be a breadwinner.

He dealt with dissatisfied bosses, machine operators,
negotiating union leaders, and belligerent labour.
Times when Naxalite ideology flourished, with
furrowed brow, and untiring effort, he kept us safe,
paid for a convent education for three daughters,
kept an eye on suitors, kept all others at bay,
let us daughters learn life lessons yet was always there.

When Mom's stroke made life for them so difficult
he agreed to shift home and country
so that her last paralyzed days were better
in the homes of her daughters and babes.
Making up for times that were spent on billiards and bridge
he then spared no effort to be by Bella's side till the end

• Serina D'Cruz Lewis •

{Contd.} Last Effort

lending a hand to feed and support her unsteady steps
and keep her company both day and night.

Through his lonely days and years after she left us
he penned many pages with tales from days gone
that were printed and bound for future generations.
He learned new rhythms, mastered the game
of bridge, and sought peace living each day
with three generations under the same roof.

When cancerous cells gnawed and corrupted,
his vulnerable body felt burdensome,
he labored for breath for hours,
 while I listened to the raspy sound
of air passing into and out of tired lungs.

Suddenly the room was quiet,
and there it was again,
his last effort to breathe, a pause,
and I heard it again.
"There's still a heartbeat," the attentive nurse declared.
With one hand in his and the other on his head
"It's ok Dad, you can fly away now", I said.
His body gave in, and I knew it was finally effortless.

{07} My Mother's Hands

a memory of hands that
bathed and bundled,
cradled and cuddled
dug deep into pockets when times were tough
encircled our faces with loving caresses
fixed buttons and bows to make us look pretty
grafted stems of roses in her prized garden
hugged us closely
idle they never were;
joined them in prayer
knitted woollies in winter,
lifted us onto rickshaws
massaged our heads with coconut oil
nursed our boo-boos with mercurochrome
organized the place meticulously
pinched us when we giggled in Church
quilted covers from leftover fabric
rapped bare bottoms as we squirmed in the shower
sewed frocks for each special occasion
tucked us into bed
used those hands to smack us when needed
vice-like grip to keep us in our place
waved us on our way when the time came
x-tended a helping hand generously
yanked on things when irritated,
zipped it when she felt defeated

when a stroke struck   those weak fingers twisted
I trimmed her nails with care   frail fingers in mine
some things are totally   out of our hands

• Serina D'Cruz Lewis •

{08} The Braid

intertwined are the
memories of childhood
in the strands that
were divided into three
neatly separated
then made into a plait

gentle hands that combed
a head full of tresses
later crooked and gnarled
unable to grasp or grip
but reaching out always
towards a miracle
after a stroke—
of misfortune

hair once long
tended with care
cut short to
a bob they called it
the hair now kept
among my souvenirs
with faded pink bow
bringing a cascade of
tingles down my spine
shivers that signal
a presence between
braider and the braid
that were never separated

{08} Singer

Black with a gold monogram
that contained the letter 'S'
for Serina? Or Singer?
It remained gold and shiny
for as long as I remember
The machine rested on a wooden base
and when Mum lifted off
the hardboard cover
we knew the magic would begin.

She'd tip the machine back to check
the bobbin, thread needle, adjust the tension
to match the fabric
With her agile toe on the motor
her right hand on the wheel
it began to sing as it rolled on
to create something special.

The base contained the bobbin
the little piece of lint-free
fabric and machine oil to grease
the electrical engine that turned
out shirts and skirts
frocks and frills
collars and cuffs
fit pieces for a runway.

Every cloth pinned and tacked
according to a pattern
that she'd craft herself

{Contd.} Singer

on yesterday's newspaper
Every turn and twist of the master's baton
would change the silks and satin
and cotton into a fashion statement
for her three girls and a generation later
her malgodi's little Anysha Angel and Divi Doll.

For decades she rolled into bundles
remnants of fabric sorted by colour or pattern
to be squared and pieced together for
a patchwork blanket,
an heirloom so cherished
a memory maker
a conversation starter
that begins (with the inevitable)
 "Do you remember that
pillow, pyjama, cushion cover,
coat, dress, or drape …?"

and the Singer's quilted song goes on ♪ ♪♪♪

{09} Elocution

At St Joseph's Convent,
Chandannagar.

In my school days, I had to learn
'by heart' poems in my reader.
The love of the lines that
had both rhythm and rhyme
was the starting point
of my love for the written word.

The very words 'by heart'
indicate for sure
that though the head was involved
it was the heart
that reigned here.

'Where the mind is without fear'
and every voice is heard
'where words come out
from the depth of truth'
of every girl's experience.

For participation in elocution
competition, each little one
in blue and white uniform
repeated every word by rote.
The Highwayman came to life
as he rode his horse each day
'tlot-tlot' into our classroom
'tlot-tlot- into our beings.

{Contd.} Elocution

The entire class of thirty in unison
would practice over and over
till we could hear just one voice.

The love of poetry
that united us as rivals
has become what now sustains
me through some difficult hours.

Who knew that I would record
memories and compose,
using couplet, quatrain, or octaves?

Who would have guessed
that I would begin to
pour on paper what today
flows from my heart
to yours?

{10} Leaving a Mark

many words were Anglicized
worship was Christianized
ways of dressing Westernized
spicy food was modified

but genes do not hide the truth
      all burnished shades of brown
tongues twist deftly around
      numerous vernacular languages
luscious lips leave one
      hungering for a little more
large shapely eyes tell tales
      of mysterious Eastern eroticism
dark tresses neatly braided
      scented flowers entwined
bare feet with jingling anklets
      beating time to haunting rhythms

hundreds of years left a mark
but the thousands before them
cannot erase the life and love
of a people and their culture

{11} What's in a Name?

Serina Mathilda Teresa D'Cruz Lewis
Serina
I heard it daily
before I made memories
Serina- quiet calm peaceful
what I was meant to be
Taken from archaic Latin
chosen by Indian parents
in a colony established
where avatars appeared

Born on the feast of a saint
a day before the ides of March
Mathilda
my middle name
from a saint alien to my roots

Grounded in Catholicism
I chose the name Teresa
from the Little Flower of Lisieux
inspired to live "the little way"
with a simple spirituality
the wildflower in the bouquet

Ancestors likely converted
long ago to Christianity
My soul took birth in a family
that was 'of the Cross'— da Cruz
Portuguese Catholic colonizers
christened families and neighbours naming a *vaddo* accordingly

{11} What's in a Name?

I fell in love with a good man
whose ancestors like mine
were named Lewis by *goras*
Assimilating with the British Raj
meant a livelihood and perks
being identified as Anglo-Indian
hyphenated with a new identity

What's in her name?
I can hear them thinking
the quick double-glance
at a noticeably brown PoC
an unidentifiable accent
with a Caucasian name

• Serina D'Cruz Lewis •

{12} Chai

In this place smells and tastes
are braided together with memories
of post-colonial daily rituals.
Water begins to boil on the gas stove
grated ginger gives the sharpness of spice
cinnamon sticks bob around
cardamom pods circulate
aromas fill the nostrils with nostalgia.
Darjeeling black tea leaves begin to move
like a convection current being carefully traced.
The color deepens as the potency percolates.
Watch it—not too long, not too soon.
Milk lightens the darkness of the blend.
It is now light brown like the colour of my skin.
Put a lid on it, and let it simmer.
When leaves settle to the bottom
the sieve separates the sediment
of potent goodness that has shared
it's bounty and is ready to be discarded.
Sugar please—a heaped spoonful to
sweeten the stories of yesteryear
when the cook performed the ceremony of
preparing the potion that pampered our dad
on his return from a day in the machine shop
Mom poured patience and love into the cup
with a saucer below to catch the dregs of
disquietude and disappointment from
labor disputes and mechanical breakdowns.
Can masala chai be an antidote?

{13} Phuchkas of Kolkata

Animated teenagers gather around a street-food vendor
on a busy, noisy, dirty street of Kolkata.
Oblivious of the unhygienic surroundings
craving the delicious treat offered,
they circle around the phuchkawala.

> He skillfully maneuvers a couple of dried leaves
> forms a cone kept in place with a tiny wooden pick
> In an aluminum bowl, he adds cubed boiled potatoes
> finely chopped onions   coriander leaves
> assortment of spices from a secret family
> formula handed down from generations.

He squishes and blends this with hands that
have scratched his back, wiped his sweaty face,
and swept up around his spot at the corner.
No one has time to question this
lest the ravenous appetite is quenched.

> Taking little crispy globes of hollowed goodness
> he punches a hole in the centre with his thumb
> fills each one with this concoction
> dipping it into the imli pani- a watery blend
> of tamarind pulp, salt, sugar, chili, cumin and
> those ingredients he has sworn never to divulge.

• Serina D'Cruz Lewis •

{Contd.} Phuchkas of Kolkata

Handing them out in turn with practiced skill
he times it to precision so each young mouth
has time to savour the phuchka, sip the tasty pani
at the bottom of the leafy bowl and prepare
for another delicious mouthful to make its entry

> Round and round he went handing out his fare
> carrying on interesting conversations with
> these young ladies who patronize his business
> encouraging one round after another till
> they are all visibly satiated

I salivate at the mere memory of those
mouth-watering phuchkas of Kolkata

{14} Making Mulkatani

my family gathers around a lazy-susan
to enjoy mulkatani or khow suey
learned in Burma and passed
down from nana to mom
now to me and my girls

      this recipe traveled across oceans
      modified by succeeding generations
      ingredients often not available now
      for the preparation of this dish
      brought from the land of the pagodas

we cut the meats into
bite-size bits of deliciousness
beef, pork, chicken, and prawns,
a portion of sharp-smelling ngapi
- a paste from preserved shrimp

      when onions are chopped, we cry
      eyes watery and nose drippy
      sharp ginger tickles our taste buds
      adding garlic that chases vampires
      from our kitchen's cozy corners

the vibrant colours
in the mouth-watering soup
turmeric, chilly reds, glossy greens
and darker tinges of dry spices
simmering till it all sizzles

• Serina D'Cruz Lewis •

{Contd.} Making Mulkatani

fried, blended, inhaled, tasted
the salty, sour, spicy and sweet
infused with creamy, coconut milk
forming a bubbling broth
in the heated cauldron

oodles of boiled noodles
form the base for the soup
submerged in the curry
to be slurped noisily
and deftly with chopsticks

the toppings for garnish
yellow and white hard-boiled
eggs- chopped and sprinkled,
fried crispy brown garlic slices,
potato sticks to add a crunch

purple onions, fresh cilantro
bright red cayenne pepper
to heighten the delight
of finely chopped green chillies
tangy lemon juice squeezed over it

not much conversation is exchanged
absorbed in the contents of our bowls
fulfilled looks on our faces
wiping evidence of satisfaction
onto every discoloured napkin

{15} Garam Masala

Life would be spicier with garam masala.
Let's add the strength of cinnamon
the heady attention of cardamom
the focus of dry flowering clove
a pinch of cayenne for the boring times
half a teaspoon each of coriander and cumin
to balance the flavors of laziness and busyness
infuse bright turmeric when inflamed
with a fury of unfairness.
What would the curry of life be like
without a fair share of salt to enhance it
and a pinch of sugar to sweeten it?
Would anyone like to share
this masaledar life with me?

• Serina D'Cruz Lewis •

Interwoven

II

{16} Log kya kahenge?

We used to play in frocks and shorts on the lawn in front
      of the row houses with kids of all shapes and sizes
We used to squeal with delight at the sprinklers that got us soaking wet as
we ran
      through the sparkling sprays that made clothes cling to skin
We used to hide in trees, behind hedgerows and bushes and in dried drains
      that no longer had runoff from heavy rain showers

We didn't hear anyone remark—what will people say?

Grew out of roles that teenagers were obliged to play as we rolled up our
sleeves
      challenged the guys to sports in the evenings
Grew up needing to hide a shape that set us up to be ogled and whistled at
      just for being adolescents in a restrictive society
Grew weary of the walls that kept us enclosed and boundaries
      that barely let the light of youth be born within us

We were relentlessly reminded—what will people say?

We were women who worked hard to juggle jobs
      more skilfully than most men
We were women who straddled kids on our hips who modeled homes
      to make them palaces where we were queen
We were women who were looked at with disdain
      when it was time to get credit for being productive

We didn't say much because we thought—what will people say?

With the World Wide Web that weaves a tapestry of threads

{Contd.} Log kya kahenge?

that strengthen us to break patterns that curb and curtail
With wisdom we have gained besides wrinkles and grey hair
along life's journey that has jolted us out of being voiceless
With hearts and minds that remind us of the ups and downs
the cost of what we had to pay along the way

Must we continue to say *log kya kahenge?*

{17} In Mid-Air

On a hot sultry afternoon
when the air could be cut with a knife
we turned the doorknob with barely a circular squeak.
Out into the garden, two sisters skipped
among beds of flowers, rows of peas, green lawns,
passing the rain barrel- a large, converted tar 'drum' half-filled with water,
and along the mud-packed path that led to the guava tree.
Our nimble limbs extended like a spider, as it navigates a web.
We climbed the crooked branches of the tree, laden with
hundreds of dark green, hard, eyeball-sized, raw guavas
among the ribbed leaves that shaded us from the afternoon sun.
My sis and I climbed into the welcoming wood of the
dividing trunk and ensconced ourselves, each one in a favourite fork
that could support our lithe little bodies, making sure that we
had an unobstructed view of the mouth of the rain barrel.
With the guavas within our arms reach we began our target practice.
Ping, plop, splash, thud- the hapless fruit landed in or around
the metal container. Oohs! and aahs! and the occasional
squeal of delight was heard when one landed in the centre.
There must have been a score or more
before we saw Mom look out from the verandah.
To our dismay, she screamed with consternation as she witnessed
a potential bountiful harvest of fruit now bobbing in the water
or lying scattered in the garden beds below us.

• Serina D'Cruz Lewis •

{Contd.} In Mid-Air

"Jump", cried my sister and she landed on all fours.
I followed, but found myself hanging by my oversize panties,
from a stub of a branch, arms flailing and with pitiful cries,
unable to run, jump, or fly, waiting to be rescued by an irate parent.
My sister laughed uproariously below.
The memory of this has been stoked and embellished
by the telling and re-telling of my plight that day.
It's made a good campfire tale and brought tears
of laughter among family and friends, young and old.
"Have you heard the story of when she hung in mid-air?"

{18} Siblings

It was the usual squabble
over hairclip, book, or candy,
we argued till we were split
up to our rooms in tears.
Now it's more about ideologies,
opinions on 'matters of consequence"
seldom seeing eye to eye though
we often agree to disagree.
Will we ever think the same
or react to life similarly?
How boring to be siblings
growing more alike than different.
This much we acknowledge,
remaining close keeping our distance
is our goal, wherever we may be,
each resolving an argument thinking,
"Let the bigger one be me."

{19} We Girls

Hum theen bahen—we three sisters

grew up in tropical climes
fun-filled childhood times
scorching summer noons
earth-quenching monsoons

later we moved across the world
a new life emerged and unfurled
From Indian summers to chilling cold
new Canadian experiences unfold

We revel in the renewed vigour of spring
the melting warmth that summers bring
envelop ourselves in the colours of fall
every season is a reason to enjoy it all

    Meri doh betiya—my two daughters

    remember little of childhood days
    of desi languages or their ways
    are happy where they've been planted
    taken root and borne fruit they wanted

    strong girls are we all

    our noses always to the grind
    our feet steadfast on the road
    our eyes on the distant horizon
    our hearts take flight and soar

{20} Front Door

We were a young family
searching for a house
to build a home.
When we did, we established
the front door to stability.

Our kids were ambitious
discovering new interests
to build young dreams.
We strove to help fulfill them
while the front door stayed sturdy.

Through the ticking of time
many friends and family
enhanced and nurtured our lives.
Over months, years, and decades
the front door stayed welcoming.

Soon our fledglings left the nest
winging their way into the world
finding skies both blue and grey
when they return they find
the front door is still open.

{21} Hold-All

A canvas carrier of quilts blankets pillows
sheets neatly packed strapped buckled in
carried by a coolie dressed in red
at a bustling railway station before
we embarked on a yearly holiday
to eagerly; waiting parents and doting grandparents
      The hold-all was opened
      each quilt spread on the bunks
      of the second-class compartment
      soon covered in fine carbon dust
      from the coal-fired train engines
      that carried us from Calcutta to Bombay
      from Howrah Station to Victoria Terminus
The hold-all was once again unrolled
on the deck of the Konkan Sewak—
a ship that sailed along the sandy coast
the bedding rolled out to cushion the swept deck
on which we kids slept played tumbled swayed
as the vessel gently rocked from side to side
      Was the bulging bedroll enough to
      hold all the thrill of young hearts
      hold all the anticipation of re-unions
      hold all the excitement of a New Year
      hold all the memories still alive
      the tales and tunes,
      the rhymes and recipes,
      the hurts and heartaches,
      of the loved ones we visited

Did it hold all?

{22} Kal Boishakhi

Nor'wester
Not a movement of air
not a leaf stirring on trees
scorching noon sunshine
clammy salty skin
cumulo-nimbus clouds
gathering darkness
with bated breath Nature waits

then you come rushing
from between uttar and paschim
north and west
    wind howling
      leaf scattering
        lightning electrifying
          thunder reverberating
            rain pounding
                down   lifting palm frond roofing
                down   tossing nests and nestlings
                down   on the homeless mercilessly
                down   on dehydrated humanity

    leaving the intoxicating smell of rain on parched earth
      leaving bone-dry gullies gushing with rainwater
        leaving dust-laden leaves green and glistening
          leaving vulnerable mangoes to the elements

• Serina D'Cruz Lewis •

{Contd.} Kal Boishakhi

You depart as swiftly as you come
We kids rush under the trees to collect
booty in the frilly folds of our frocks
"Don't enter the grove it's lightning," goes unheeded
Children's defiance of a mother's warning
exercising independence at that early age

we gather the forbidden fruit
Sliced salted sour mangoes with fresh
chopped crunchy spicy green chillies

I salivate at the mere memory

{23} Waters

From life-giving water I broke out
A foetus emerged
from a dark constricted tunnel
into this bright wide world

Washed in waters
cleansed on the outside
awaiting absolution
from original transgression

Alma mater by the Indo-French
Riviera of Chandannagar
The silt laden Ganga waters
enriching the roots of knowledge

Nourished by the waters
of the Hooghly River
A humble nouka to ferry me across
to the jute mills along the banks

Sandy beaches by Arabian Sea waters
where dreams of young lovers
came to fruition in the home called
Sand Dunes of Miramar

Drawn to the southern shores
of the Bay of Bengal in Madras
where St. Thomas poured on so many
the waters of sacramental life

{Contd.} Waters

Across the world of seas
to the fresh waters of Lake Ontario
the land of Indigenous Mississaugas
to my new chosen home

Many a pensive hour I now spend
by the sparkling waters
of the Credit River through all seasons
soothing all my senses

From and in primordial waters
we are birthed, bathed, and immersed
each one a drop that eventually
merges with the ocean

{24} I Hear You Call

I hear you call, little *koel*, I hear you in hidden branches, of the groves
of mango trees, I hear your urgent call each spring, dear koel.
What is your refrain, blackbird, when dawn is bathed in spring showers
that make leaves dark and glossy, what do you respond to, lone koel?
I hear your koo-oooo, loud caller, in my dreams and do not know
which echo spurs me, red-eyed one.
When will I return home, *kali koel*?

{25} Raath ki Rani

I return to India
after a decade or more
to many familiar
sights and smells.
In the early dusk,
as the sun descends
to its resting place
below the horizon,
I breathe in the fragrance
of Raath ki Rani.
It begins to bloom
at the end of day,
when weary of bone
I climb to the terrace,
a respite from the heat
and damp of summer.
With a gentle breeze
beginning to blow
my weariness away,
soothing my soul,
I inhale the heady
scent of the white,
star-shaped blossoms
amid dark green leaves.
The senses awaken,
the memory revives
the enveloping warmth of a princess
on her mother's breast each night.
Is this what it feels like to return?
I am home.

{26} Aam Gachh - Mango Trees

Its outspreading branches above me
an umbrella in the pouring monsoons
a parasol in the blistering summer

      Its skirt of green kept secrets we shared
      under its petticoat just the two of us
      a silent immobile witness to love

Its gnarled bark is a chairback
for sweaty weary workers resting
from labour on hot afternoons

      Its luscious fruit dangling above
      beckoning neighbourhood kids
      to taste their juicy goodness

Its branches sang soothing songs
to the sad and lonely as they swayed
to the changes in the winds of time

      Charming mango trees of childhood
      now Mighty Maples as I ponder
      What tree will I next cherish
      as I inevitably grow older?

• Serina D'Cruz Lewis •

{27} Half and Half

Namaskaram

I realize that half my life
was spent in a country
far 'faaaar' away.

The elegant, exotic garb
of six yards of silken sari
drapes around a brown body.
Yes, there are many shades of brown,
potions like 'Fair and Lovely'
are a testament to the glorification of *"gora."*
White was right and signified might, for centuries.

I spent thirty-two years,
where crows caw on overhead electric wires,
cows stall traffic on busy city streets,
children with bloated bellies play with abandon,
lepers with bound limbs lean forward to beg,
delicious street foods entice young and old
Bollywood songs and calls to prayer
blare from loudspeakers.

Thirty-two years spanning
different states, and stages of life,
from a carefree childhood in a colonial estate,
to troubled teen years in a restrictive society,
in a civilization that goes back millennia
where people have migrated and assimilated.
Memories of my *jonmobhumi* or motherland

{Contd.} Half and Half

linger now where I currently stand.
They follow the winding raging rivers
like the Yamuna and the Holy Ganga,
where Himalayan silt-laden polluted waters
flood rice paddies, feed burgeoning cities.

A century ago, an adventurous great-grandfather
traversed seas to Canadian shores,
worked in the cross-country railways,
bore the travails of early immigrants.
Thirty-two years have I now spent
understanding Indigenous sentiments,
being schooled in convents
in a land far 'faaar' away.
Mesmerizing Aurora Borealis make
northern nights in Arctic climes memorable,
Pacific old-growth forests preserve in trunks
stories of tribes from long ago.
The bear, beaver, bison, and bald eagle
Canada goose, moose, loon, and squirrel
share this diverse land of ours.

The Sugar Maple and Mighty Oak,
witness the love of my chosen land.
Sky-scraping Rockies, rolling wheat fields,
crashing waves on Atlantic shores,
huddled by a campfire roasting smores-
these are new memories of not so long ago.
I stroll where the Credit River winds its way
to the lake of sparkling waters.

• Serina D'Cruz Lewis •

{Contd.} Half and Half

I listen to languages from around the globe,
taste delicious cuisines of various cultures,
along with the bitterness of racism,
ageism, sexism, and nepotism.

What makes this feel like home?
It's a sense of belonging that is traced
from an ancestor a century ago.
It's where I was destined to be.
Thirty-two years have allowed me
to build bridges bridge borders
in this land- glorious, strong, and free.

Deo borem korum.

Notes

Day of the Living
letri, bathica, dose, pinag are sweetmeats prepared for festive occasions
mandddem and *dulpodam* are kinds of folksongs of Goa

The Circle
Chappals- Flip-flops in Hindi
Sansaar- Earth in Hindi
Dhonnobad- Thanks in Bengali
Manddem- folk songs of Goa, India
Miigwich Chi Miigwich- Thanks, Many Thanks in Ojibwa

Waters
Nouka- a row boat that ferried people across the River Ganga

Singer
Malgodi means the eldest daughter in our "mother tongue" Konkani

What's in a Name?
PoC reads as a Person of Colour

Phuchkas of Kolkata
phuchka - a street food and the man who makes and serves them is a *phuchkawala*

Garam Masala
masaledar means spicy in Hindi

Making Mulkatani
Kaukswe- sounds like *khow-suey,* which we came to know as Mulkatani, and others know as *mulligatawny*- a kind of soup.

{Contd.} Notes

gnapi- is a pungent paste made of fish or shrimp, used in Burmese cooking

Log kya kahenge?
Means What will people say? in Hindi

Kal Boishakhi
Uttar - north
Paschim- west

Half and Half
Namaskaram- Respectful Greetings in Sanskrit
Gora - White Man
Deo borem korum - Thank You in Konkani

Acknowledgements

The Courtney Park Writers Group for publishing The Circle and Singer in the Crazy Cove anthology, which are included in this collection.

The Mississauga Writers Group for publishing my writing in ezines and anthologies, which I have included here: 'Raath ki Rani', 'Arranged Marriage', 'What Will People Say?'

Gratitude and Thanks

To Zilka Joseph who was one of the first to challenge and guide me on my poetry writing journey and has edited this collection.

To the staff of Visual Arts Mississauga who started a reading group during the 'pandemic days' of 2020, that gave me a glimpse into the arts—the many ways a person can express their creativity.

To the Mississauga Writers Group and the Courtney Park Writers Group who opened me to the world of possibilities in writing.

To Rudi Rodrigues, Creative Director Avatar Inc. who read the collection and designed a cover to reflect it.

To Deanne who lent creative hands to the expressive cover.

To Zohra Zoberi who encouraged me to compile a collection of my poems to share with the world and has written a great review of my first complete publication.

To Sheila Tucker who inspires me with her passion for the written word and has written a wonderful review for this book.

To Emma, Rubina and Ryan D'Souza who read an early version of this collection and were excited.

To Noel Lewis, whose responses ranged from 'nice' to 'very nice' and who has supported me through all the creative spurts and lulls.

To my family, who are the inspiration behind many of these poems, read the early compositions, and agreed to read some more.

To friends from around the world who have given me valuable feedback.

Printed in the USA
CPSIA information can be obtained
at www.ICGtesting.com
JSHW021015141024
71604JS00002B/77